The Importance of Health and Hygiene in Islam

عناية الإسلام بالصحة والنظافة

اللغة الانجليزية

By
Dr. Muhammad bin Ibrahim Al-Hamad

تأليف د. محمد بن إبراهيم الحمد

Importance of Health and Hygiene in Islam

Section One: Public Health in Islam

The importance of health in Islam and its preservation of physical and mental health has already been touched upon under discussion of the benefits of having belief in the six pillars of faith as well as under the discussion of the pillars of Islam. This topic has also been addressed in other chapters such as the harms and ill-effects of sin on the wellbeing of a person. The following pages will aim to complete and supplement what has been previously mentioned regarding the subject.

Firstly: Islam recommends moderation in eating and drinking: This is something which is self-evident. Just as deprivation or abstinence from food and drink can cause illness, and ultimately, death, excessive eating and drinking can also cause various diseases. Moderation is thus what preserves health and, by the permission of Allah, helps prevent disease. Allah the Almighty says:

Sura al-A'raf; (7):31 ﴿ وَكُلُوا۟ وَٱشْرَبُوا۟ وَلَا تُسْرِفُوٓا۟ ﴾

[Meaning: And eat and drink but be not excessive.]

Some of the scholars have said regarding this verse: "Allah summed up in these words all of medicine."[1]
Similar to the meaning of this verse is the narration of the Prophet ﷺ wherein he warns against gluttony by saying: "No human ever filled a vessel worse than their stomach. Sufficient for the children of Adam are a few morsels to sustain them. If one must, then they should reserve one third for food, one third for drink and one third for breathing."[2]

Secondly: There are many Islamic rulings which ensure the preservation of health:
For example, Islam forbids alcohol which is harmful to the health of a person in many ways, such as by weakening the heart and destroying the kidneys and liver.
Moreover, Islam forbids fornication and homosexuality which also have their dangers. Many diseases such as syphilis, gonorrhoea, herpes, and AIDS have spread in recent times due to these practices.
Furthermore, Islam prohibits the consumption of pork, which is now known to cause many diseases such as taeniasis, cysticercosis, and trichinosis. The

---

[1] See: *'Tadhkirat as-Sami' wal-Mutakallim'* of Ibn Jama'ah (p. 121).
[2] Reported by Ahmad (4/132) & al-Hakim (4/121) and authenticated by al-Albani in *'as-Sahihah'* (no. 2265) and in *'Sahih al-Jami"* (no. 5674).

parasitic worms contained in pork have devastating effects on humans which often lead to death.[3]

Among the rulings of Islam which ensure the preservation of health is ablution which helps to prevent diseases of the teeth and nose, as well as tuberculosis, which some doctors say is contracted primarily via the nose. They also point out that if a person's nose is washed up to fifteen times a day, it is highly unlikely that any bacteria responsible for causing this infection will remain. For this reason, tuberculosis is much more prevalent in the West than it is among Muslims, as they are obliged be in a state of ritual purity for their five daily prayers which means they perform ablution and wash their nostrils one, twice or thrice for each prayer.[4]

The benefits of ablution will be further elaborated later on.

Thirdly: Islam advises seeking medical treatment for health problems and illnesses:

Allah the Almighty says:

﴿ مِنْ أَجْلِ ذَٰلِكَ كَتَبْنَا عَلَىٰ بَنِىٓ إِسْرَٰٓءِيلَ أَنَّهُۥ مَن قَتَلَ نَفْسًۢا بِغَيْرِ نَفْسٍ أَوْ فَسَادٍ فِى ٱلْأَرْضِ فَكَأَنَّمَا قَتَلَ ٱلنَّاسَ جَمِيعًا وَمَنْ أَحْيَاهَا فَكَأَنَّمَآ أَحْيَا

---

[3] See: 'Ta'rif 'Aam bi Din al-Islam al-Musamma bi Rasa·il al-Islam wa Rusul as-Salam' (pp. 38-9).
[4] See: 'Ta'rif 'Aam bi Din al-Islam' (p. 45) & 'at-Tariq Ilal-Islam' (pp. 35-6).

﴿ٱلنَّاسَ جَمِيعًا ۚ وَلَقَدْ جَآءَتْهُمْ رُسُلُنَا بِٱلْبَيِّنَٰتِ ثُمَّ إِنَّ كَثِيرًا مِّنْهُم بَعْدَ ذَٰلِكَ فِى ٱلْأَرْضِ لَمُسْرِفُونَ﴾

Sura al-Ma·idah; (5):32

[Meaning: Because of that, We decreed upon the Children of Israel that whoever kills a soul not in retaliation of murder or for corruption done in the land, then it is as if he had killed all of humankind. And whoever saves one life - it is as if they had saved humankind entirely. And our messengers had certainly come to them with clear proofs. Then indeed many of them, even after that, were transgressors throughout the land.]

The significance of this verse is that Allah the Almighty praised the one who strives to save a life and rescue them from death, which is one of the primary goals of medicine. Medicine treats serious health conditions which, if left untreated could result in death, and thus saves lives by the permission of Allah. This contains an indication of the virtue of medicine and its excellence.[5]

Fourthly: Evidence permitting surgery:

There are various Prophetic traditions which indicate the permissibility of medical surgery, such as the narrations concerning cupping. For instance, Ibn 'Abbas – may Allah be pleased with him and his

---

[5] See: '*Ahkam al-Jirahah at-Tibbiyyah wal-Aathar al-Mutarattibah 'Alaiha*' of Dr Muhammad al-Mukhtar ash-Shanqiti (pp. 85-6).

father – relates that the Prophet ﷺ had bloodletting performed on his head.⁶ Another example is the narration wherein Jabir bin 'Abdullah – may Allah be pleased with him – visited a sick man and said to him: 'Why do you not have bloodletting performed on you, for I heard Allah's Messenger ﷺ say: "There is healing in bloodletting."'⁷ These narrations permit the practice of bloodletting, which involves making an incision in a specific part of the body and extraction of bad blood by way of suction. By way of deduction, it is possible to conclude the permissibility of making surgical incisions in the body for the purpose of removing diseased organs, cysts, tumours and the like.⁸ Furthermore, bloodletting is considered in modern medical terms to be a minor surgical procedure and is used to treat certain illnesses and infections.⁹

Another piece of evidence proving the permissibility of surgical procedures in Islam is the narration of Jabir bin 'Abdullah – may Allah be pleased with him and his father – wherein he mentions that Allah's Messenger ﷺ sent a doctor to Ubayy bin Ka'b who cut one of his veins and then cauterised it."¹⁰ The significance of this narration is that the Prophet ﷺ approved of the doctor's practice. Cutting a vein is a

---

⁶ Reported by al-Bukhari (no. 5373).
⁷ Reported by al-Bukhari (no. 5372).
⁸ See: '*Ahkam al-Jirahah at-Tibbiyyah*' (p. 88).
⁹ See: '*al-Jirahah as-Sughra*' of Dr. Ridwan Babuli and Dr. Antoine Duli (p. 24).
¹⁰ Reported by Muslim (no. 2207).

form of surgical treatment which is still used today, for instance in cases of arteriovenous blockages or lesions.[11]

There are many other narrations in this regard.[12]

Fifthly: Prophet Muhammad ﷺ encouraged people to study medicine and advance in it:

This is clearly demonstrated in the saying of the Prophet ﷺ: "Allah did not send down any disease except that He sent down its cure."[13] 'Allah did not send down' means: 'He did not decree'. Shaikh 'Abdur-Rahman as-Sa'di – may Allah have mercy upon him – commented on this narration, saying: "The generality of this narration implies that there are remedies for the treatment of all internal diseases, some of which are preventive while others are either partially or fully curative. It thus contains an incentive for people to study medicine as a useful means of treatment just as they study faith healing. All of the detailed information regarding medicine is merely an explanation of this narration because Allah mentions that all diseases have cures, and thus people must strive to study and implement them."[14]

---

[11] See: '*Ahkam al-Jirahah at-Tibbiyyah*' (p. 88).
[12] See the chapters on medicine in the authentic collections of Prophetic traditions for further narrations.
[13] Reported by al-Bukhari (no. 5354).
[14] '*Bahjat Qulub al-Abrar fi Sharh Jawami' al-Akhbar*' of Shaikh 'Abdur-Rahman as-Sa'di (pp. 213-4).

Moreover, this narration clearly indicates that there is no reason to despair of the cure for any illness, since Allah is Causer of causes and He did not create a disease except that He created its cure.

Many people used to consider certain diseases incurable, however, with the progression of medicine and its development, they came to learn the truthfulness of this narration.[15]

Sixthly: Contributions of Muslim scholars to the field of medicine

Europe in the Middle Ages lived under the grip of ignorance and underwent a period of stagnation. At the same time, Islamic civilisation was flourishing with advancements in many fields to the extent that foreigners, particularly from Europe, would travel to the lands of Islam to study the various branches of knowledge which the Muslims had progressed significantly in.

The Muslim scholars of the Islamic Golden Age made impressive contributions to many fields including medicine, mathematics and astronomy. Their intellects were fortified with the Quran and Prophetic traditions, and due to this they were the driving force behind scientific progress and research in their era.[16]

Shaikh Muhammad Al-Mukhtar Ash-Shanqiti – may Allah preserve him – writes in this regard: "The

---

[15] See: *'Bahjat Qulub al-Abrar'* (p. 214).
[16] See: *'Ahkam al-Jirahah at-Tibbiyyah'* (p. 50).

Muslim scholars of the Islamic Golden Age excelled in all specialities of medicine, including surgery, as well as many other branches of knowledge. Surgery was initially a profession which Muslim doctors looked down upon and did not engage in. They described it as manual labour and saw it as belonging to bloodletters who would perform cauterisation, bleeding, cupping and amputations under the supervision and instruction of doctors.

However, as time progressed, surgery became much more advanced and demanded a much higher level of skill and precision, thanks to the grace of Allah and then to the various sincere efforts of such scholars."[17]
He adds: "They were the first to dedicate sections of their books to surgery and they were also the first to devote entire books to this subdiscipline, which they wrote in a wonderful, academic style based on the knowledge they had acquired previously. In these works, they meticulously recorded the various medical procedures they pioneered, such as:

1. Lithotomies, which are a surgical method for removal of calculi, or bladder stones.
2. Nasal fracture surgery.
3. Tracheotomies, or tracheostomies, which refer to the surgical procedure wherein an incision is made on the anterior aspect of the neck and a direct airway is

---

[17] See: *'Ahkam al-Jirahah at-Tibbiyyah'* (pp. 50-1).

opened through an incision in the trachea to relieve obstructions to breathing.

4. Tonsillectomies, which refer to the surgical procedure in which both palatine tonsils are fully removed from the back of the throat.

5. Draining peritonsillar abscesses.

6. Removal of aural polyps.

7. Otitis media, or middle ear infection.

In addition to these discoveries, they were also the first to discuss various issues pertinent to surgery, such as the difference between malignant, or cancerous, tumours and benign, non-cancerous tumours. They recorded some of the symptoms in order to help doctors reach correct diagnoses of patients; if a tumour was malignant then it was to be avoided, whereas benign tumours could be surgically removed."[18]

Shaikh Muhammad Al-Mukhtar Ash-Shanqiti – may Allah preserve him – goes on to list many examples of Muslim doctors who pioneered in various subdisciplines of medicine, such as Avenzoar[19] and

---

[18] See: '*Ahkam al-Jirahah at-Tibbiyyah*' (pp. 50-1).

[19] 'Abdul-Malik bin Zuhr was born somewhere between the years 484-487 AH and he died in 557 AH. He is considered to be the first surgeon to have precisely described a tracheotomy in his great book '*at-Taysir fil-Mudawati wat-Tadbir*' (Book of Simplification Concerning Therapeutics and Diet). See: '*Ahkam al-Jirahah at-Tibbiyyah*' (p. 53).

Rhazes[20]. He proceeds to discuss Abulcasis and his works and contributions to the fields of medicine and surgery at length, mentioning that Abulcasis had an enormous impact on physicians and surgeons as far away as Europe for centuries after his death.

Ash-Shanqiti comments on one of Abulcasis' works on the topic of surgery, wherein he describes many new types of surgery and surgical inventions. Ash-Shanqiti goes on to speak of the specific surgical procedures of Abdulcasis, including his revolutionary technique of lithotomy, as well as surgeries of the eye, ear, throat, mouth, teeth, and jaw. He mentions Abulcasis' treatments for hernias and what is known as goitre, which is a swelling of the thyroid gland.[21] Ash-Shanqiti concludes his discussion by recalling scholarly praise of Abulcasis, quoting the likes of Dr Simon Hayek who wrote the following: "Guy de Chauliac (1300-1367) was the first of a long series of French surgeons influenced by Abulcasis. He studied in Boulogne, France, taught in Montpellier and then joined the Pop's Court in Avignon. He wrote a book: *'La Pratique en Chirurgie'* printed in Lyon in 1478.

---

[20] Abu Bakr Muhammad bin Zakariyyah ar-Razi was born in 254 AH and died in Baghdad in the year 311 AH. He was the first person to discuss the difference between venous and arterial haemorrhages, and he proposed various methods of stopping arterial haemorrhages. He also made valuable contributions to the field of bone fracture repair and surgery. See: '*Ahkam al-Jirahah at-Tibbiyyah*' (p. 53).

[21] See: '*Aham al-Jirahah at-Tibbiyyah*' (pp. 54-65).

As for the original Latin version, it was printed in Venice in 1490 and had great influence on the subsequent surgeons as it advised to stop using insecticides and to return to the use of ointments oils and lints following in this way the steps of Abulcasis."[22]

Abulcasis' influence continued long after his death, despite the fact he died during the eleventh century, over a millennium ago, in Andalusia.[23]

Seventhly: Jurists consider health preservation to be one of the objectives of Islamic legislation.

All the laws of Islam give importance to bodily health and wellbeing and consider it from the fundamental purposes behind Islamic rulings. It is for this reason that asking Allah for good health is considered to be from the best of supplications, being surpassed in importance only by the blessing of faith. Prophet Muhammad ﷺ said: "Ask Allah for certainty and wellbeing, for verily nobody has been granted anything better than wellbeing."[24] From the supplications of the Prophet ﷺ was that he would say: "O Allah, grant me health in my body; O Allah grant

---

[22] See: '*Ahkam al-Jirahah at-Tibbiyyah*' (p. 65).
[23] See: 'Jadhwatul-Muqtabas' of al-Humaydi (pp. 208-9) & '*Ahkam al-Jirahah at-Tibbiyyah*' (p. 55).
[24] Reported by at-Tirmidhi (no. 3558) and graded by al-Albani as: 'Good, authentic' in '*Sahih wa Da'if Sunan at-Tirmidhi*' (no. 3558).

Health and Hygiene in Islam

me good hearing; O Allah grant me good eyesight. There is no god in truth but You."[25]

Dr Muhammad Nizar Ad-Daqar writes: "The outlook of Islam on health corresponds to the modern conception of health. Modern medicine considers health to be a reserve of strength which allows a person to perform bodily functions and withstand disease and not merely the absence of disease or infirmity. This corresponds miraculously with the saying of Prophet Muhammad ﷺ: 'The strong believer is better and more beloved to Allah than the weak believer.'[26]"[27]

Eighthly: Islam ensures the good health of humans even before they are born by advising spouses to choose their partner while having consideration for the health of their children. Prophet Muhammad ﷺ says: "Choose the best for your seed."[28]

Furthermore, Islam encourages breastfeeding for as long as possible so that children receive antibodies which they would not otherwise get. Allah the Almighty says:

---

[25] Reported by Abu Dawud (no. 5090) and graded by al-Albani as having 'a good chain of narration' in '*Sahih Abi Dawud*' (no. 5090).

[26] Reported by Muslim (no. 2664).

[27] See: '*Rawa·i' at-Tibb al-Islamiyy*' of Dr. Muhammad Nizar ad-Daqar (1/2).

[28] Reported by Ibn Majah (no. 1968) and declared by al-Albani to be authentic in '*as-Sahihah*' (no. 1067).

﴿ وَٱلْوَٰلِدَٰتُ يُرْضِعْنَ أَوْلَٰدَهُنَّ حَوْلَيْنِ كَامِلَيْنِ ﴾

Sura al-Baqarah; (2):233

[Meaning: The mothers shall give suck to their children for two whole years.][29]

Ninthly: Islam prescribes certain remedies and directs people to certain cures. For example, Prophet Muhammad ﷺ says: "Use black caraway, for it contains a cure from every illness."[30]

The Quran encourages with preventive healthcare, which consists of taking measures to prevent disease. Allah the Almighty says:

﴿ وَلَا تُلْقُوا بِأَيْدِيكُمْ إِلَى ٱلتَّهْلُكَةِ ﴾ Sura al-Baqarah; (2):195

[Meaning: And make not your own hands contribute to your destruction.]

Islamic legislation was likely the first to prescribe the globally adopted health practice of quarantine in times of epidemics such as the plague and cholera. In a narration referenced by the two canonical collections of Prophetic traditions, Al-Bukhari and Muslim, guidelines which are now recognised by modern medicine are provided for quarantine. Prophet

---

[29] See: *'Rawa·i' at-Tibb al-Islamiyy'* of Dr. Muhammad Nizar ad-Daqar (1/3).

[30] See: *'Rawa·i' at-Tibb al-Islamiyy'* of Dr. Muhammad Nizar ad-Daqar (1/3).

Muhammad ﷺ said: "Plague is a calamity which was inflicted on those who were before you. So, if there is an outbreak in a land while you are in it, then do not leave it in an attempt to flee from it, and if news reaches you that it has spread in a land, then do not enter it."[31]

Dr Muhammad Ad-Daqar writes in commentary of the foregoing narration: "Those who know the importance of quarantine in public health are aware of just how much healthcare in Islam has contributed to the preservation of humanity."[32]

Tenthly: Islamic etiquette regarding food and drink contains many indications of health promotion.

Dr Muhammad Ad-Daqar writes: "Islamic rules relating to food are just one example of the excellent teachings of Prophet Muhammad ﷺ. They ensure Muslims consume clean, uncontaminated food by ordering them to eat with their right hands; to wash their hands before and after eating; not to eat excessively and to space meals out."

He continues: "One of the main objectives which Allah the Almighty entrusted Muhammad ﷺ with is to make lawful everything good and beneficial and to prohibit everything evil and harmful. When

---

[31] Reported by al-Bukhari (no. 5398) and Muslim (no. 2218). The wording mentioned here is that of Musim.
[32] See: *'Rawa·i' at-Tibb al-Islamiyy'* (1/3).

mentioning the objectives of Muhammad's mission, Allah says:

﴿ وَيُحِلُّ لَهُمُ ٱلطَّيِّبَـٰتِ وَيُحَرِّمُ عَلَيْهِمُ ٱلْخَبَـٰٓئِثَ ﴾

Sura al-A'raf; (7):157

[Meaning: He permits for them whatever is good and pure, and he forbids them from whatever is evil and harmful.]"[33]

He proceeds to write: "The prohibition of alcohol, smoking and narcotics may be considered as one of the most significant accomplishments of the noble religion of Islam with regards to preventive healthcare. In fact, if a society were to abstain from all evil and harmful matters it would be safe from many deadly diseases and there would be a reduction in birth defects, as well as a decrease in the number of accidents."[34]

Eleventhly: Islamic law has prescribed certain rules in order to prevent the occurrence of accidents which lead to loss of life or harm of others. These come in the form of clear commands and prohibitions which ensure safety while preventing damage. Examples include the prohibition of stopping in the middle of a road. Abu Hurairah narrates the saying of the Prophet ﷺ: "When you camp late, then stay away from roads, for they are frequented by noxious creatures at night."

---

[33] See: 'Rawa·i' at-Tibb al-Islamiyy' (1/4).
[34] See: 'Rawa·i' at-Tibb al-Islamiyy' (1/4).

A variant narration states: "When you camp at night, then stay away from the road, for indeed it is the route of the beasts and the abode of noxious creatures."[35]
Further examples include the prohibition of sleeping on an unfenced roof terrace[36] and the prohibition of sleeping while a fire is still lit. The Prophet ﷺ said: "Do not leave a fire burning in your houses when you go to sleep."[37]

The foregoing has been but a short overview of health and its importance in Islam. This discussion will be continued in the following section on hygiene in Islam.

---

[35] Reported by Muslim (no. 1926).
[36] Reported by Abu Dawud (no. 5041).
[37] Reported by al-Bukhari (no. 5935) and Muslim (no. 2015).

Hygiene in Islam

Section Two: Hygiene in Islam

Several parts of this treatise have touched upon the topic of hygiene in Islam. In this section, hygiene will be discussed further in light of the narration regarding the traits of the natural disposition of a person. Consideration will also be given to ablution, bathing and public hygiene. It should be noted that what follows serves only as a brief glimpse into hygiene in Islam.

Firstly: The narration mentioning the traits of a person's innate disposition

On the authority of Aisha – may Allah be pleased with her – that Allah's Messenger ﷺ said: "Ten things are from the innate disposition of a person: trimming the moustache; growing the beard; brushing the teeth; washing the nostrils; clipping the nails; washing the finger joints; plucking the armpits; shaving pubic hair and cleansing the private parts with water." The narrator said: 'I forgot the tenth, but it was possibly rinsing the mouth.'[38]

This narration contains a valuable set of recommendations related to hygiene which are

---

[38] Reported by Muslim (no. 216).

associated as being from the innate disposition, or the natural inclination which Allah placed in people, whereby He created them having a love for good and a dislike for evil.

The traits of a person's innate disposition can be categorised into two main categories in the following manner:

I. Traits which ensure spiritual purification of the heart and soul, such as faith and its corollaries, which purify the soul and cleanse the heart by ridding them of vices and encouraging virtues.

II. Traits which ensure physical purification of the body and its cleanliness. These traits consist of a person ridding themselves of everything which may defile the body, and it is this category which is the subject of the foregoing narration.[39]

Each of the ten traits will now be explored in turn.

1. Trimming the moustache, i.e. shortening it so that the upper lip is visible. This is a hygiene measure to prevent any nasal discharge from entering the mouth and it ensures that the moustache is not in contact with any food or drink. In addition to being

---

[39] See: '*Sahih Muslim*' with the explanation of an-Nawawi (3/149) & '*Bahjat Qulub al-Abrar fi Sharh Jawami' al-Akhbar*' of Shaikh 'Abdur-Rahman as-Sa'di (p. 81).

unhygienic, an overly long moustache is also unsightly.[40]

Dr Muhammad Ad-Daqar writes: "From a medical perspective, a long moustache is considered to be unhygienic because it comes into constant contact with food and drink and therefore, can easily spread germs." He continues: "The Islamic prescription of trimming the moustache conforms to the recommendation of modern medicine to remove whatever overhangs the upper lip."[41]

2. **Growing the beard,** i.e. maintaining it and not shaving it.

Shaikh 'Abdur-Rahman as-Sa'di – may Allah have mercy upon him – comments on this, saying: "Allah made the beard a symbol of solemnity and beauty for men, and it is because of the beard that a man remains handsome in old age."[42]

Dr 'Abdur-Razzaq Kaylani is of the opinion that men's exposure to the sun's rays and the elements whilst working can cause damage to the elastic fibres and collagen found in facial skin, which in turn can lead to the appearance of wrinkles and premature ageing.[43]

---

[40] See: *'Bahjat Qulub al-Abrar fi Sharh Jawami' al-Akhbar'* (p. 82).
[41] See: *'Rawa·i' at-Tibb al-Islamiyy'* (1/73-4).
[42] See: *'Bahjat Qulub al-Abrar'* (p. 82).
[43] *'Rawa·i' at-Tibb al-Islaamiyy'* (1/74).

Health and Hygiene in Islam

3. Brushing the teeth, i.e. cleansing the teeth by use of a twig or similar object in order to rid the mouth of plaque and remnants of food.[44]

A person may brush their teeth at any time, but this practice is strongly recommended at the times of ablution, prayer, awakening, bad breath, build-up of plaque and the like.

When a person brushes their teeth, they are cleansing and purifying their mouth which is the part of the body they use to communicate. It is also the route most bacteria enter the body via, and this is why Prophet Muhammad ﷺ associated cleanliness of the mouth with the pleasure of Allah in his saying: "Brushing the teeth cleanses the mouth and pleases the Lord."[45]

4. Washing the nostrils, i.e. when a person washes out their nose by snuffing water and blowing it out at the time of ablution or bathing. Cleaning the nostrils is an obligation in both of these acts as they contain mucus, debris and other impurities which a person must rid them of.[46] In addition to it being an act of hygiene, washing the nostrils is also a source of reward and good deeds.

---

[44] See: '*Lisan al-Arab*' (10/446) & '*Sahih Muslim*' with the explanation of an-Nawawi (3/142).
[45] Reported by ash-Shafi'i in '*al-Umm*' (1/23) and Ahmad (6/47, 62, 124).
[46] See: '*Bahjat Qulub al-Abrar*' (p. 81).

The author of '*Asbab Ash-Shifa· Min Al-Asqam Wal-Ahwa·* (The Means to Cure Illness and Desires)' writes: "Recent research carried out by a team of doctors from Alexandria University reveals that people who regularly perform ablution have been found to have clean noses which are free of debris, bacteria and germs. It is well known that the nasal cavity is a reservoir for bacteria and germs, however continuous washing of the nostrils by snuffing water and forcefully blowing it out cleans the nasal cavity and causes it to be inflammation- and germ-free. This in turn leads to an improvement in physical health in general since there is less risk of microbes being transferred from the nose to other parts of the body."[47]

5. Clipping the nails, i.e. shortening or cutting them, as occurs in variant narrations.[48] Trimming the nails undoubtedly protects against bacteria which form under long nails.

6. Washing the finger joints, An-Nawawi – may Allah have mercy upon him – said: "Finger joint refers to the creases between each of the finger segments. The scholars have mentioned that this ruling is also to be applied to all parts of the body which have creases or folds in the skin. This includes the ears which, left uncleaned, accumulate wax and

---

[47] See: '*Asbab ash-Shifa· minal-Asqam wal-Ahwa·*' of Abu Ishaq al-'Iraqi' (p. 40).
[48] See: '*Sahih Muslim*' (no. 257).

can cause loss of hearing. Likewise, the inside of the nose and any other part of the body where sweat, grime and other impurities gather, and Allah knows best."[49]

7. Plucking the armpits, i.e. removal of axillary hair. An-Nawawi – may Allah have mercy upon him – commented on this, saying: "Removing underarm hair is from the Prophetic way according to the consensus of Islamic scholars. It is better that axillary hair is plucked if a person can bear the pain, however it is also permissible to remove it by shaving."[50]

8. Shaving pubic hair, i.e. the hair around a man's penis and a woman's vagina, as well as the hair around the anus.[51] An-Nawawi – may Allah have mercy upon him – writes in this regard: "What is to be deduced from this is the recommendation of shaving genital and anal hair, as well as the area surrounding them. These regions should be shaved as frequently as is necessary. This rule also applies to trimming the moustache, plucking the armpits and clipping the nails. The narration of Anas wherein he states that 'We were given a time limit with regard to trimming the moustache, shaving pubic hair, plucking axillary

---

[49] See: '*Sahih Muslim*' with the explanation of an-Nawawi (3/150).
[50] See: '*Sahih Muslim*' with the explanation of an-Nawawi (3/149).
[51] See: '*Sahih Muslim*' with the explanation of an-Nawawi (3/148).

hair and clipping nails'[52] means that a person must not leave these acts for more than forty days, not that the frequency of these acts is fixed at forty days, and Allah knows best."[53]

This practice is undoubtedly one which promotes sophistication, hygiene, cleanliness, health and comfort.

Regarding the benefits of plucking axillary hair, Dr Kaylani writes: "Plucking reduces the secretions of sweat and sebaceous glands. Habitually plucking hair as soon as it begins to appear, without ever resorting to shaving it, weakens hair and, in time, leads to painless plucking. The hair should be removed by hand or by using depilatory creams.

The appearance of axillary hair at puberty is accompanied by the development of apocrine glands which produce odorous secretions which are broken down and, when mixed with grime and dirt, leads to unpleasant body odour. Plucking underarm hair greatly reduces body odour and decreases the risk of skin diseases of the axillary region such as intertrigo, fungal infections, hidradenitis suppurativa and folliculitis. It also prevents parasitic infestations such as pubic lice."[54]

---

[52] Reported by Muslim (no. 258).
[53] See: *'Sahih Muslim'* with the explanation of an-Nawawi (3/148-9).
[54] See: *'Rawa·i' at-Tibb al-Islaamiyy'* (1/72).

Dr Muhammad Nizar Ad-Daqar discusses the wisdom of this Islamic prescription and mentions the hygiene and health benefits associated with removing pubic hair, saying: "The pubic and perianal regions are prone to heavy perspiration and chafing, and if they are not depilated, oil and sebum can accumulate. Matters are made worse when there are traces of urine and excrement, as they make it more difficult to clean such regions of the body. These impurities may affect neighbouring areas and their further accumulation can lead to fermentation and foul odours. If such filth is left uncleaned, it may reach a stage whereby a person's prayer is invalid."

Dr Ad-Daqar goes on to mention the benefits of shaving pubic hair, saying: "Shaving pubic hair also helps to prevent numerous parasitic diseases such as pubic lice, or crabs, which live at the roots of the hair and are thus difficult to get rid of. Shaving pubic hair also reduces the risk of fungal infections. It is for these reasons that Islam prescribed shaving pubic and perianal hair whenever it becomes long; in order to ensure hygiene and because these areas of the body are the most susceptible to dirt and diseases."[55]

9. **Cleansing the private parts,** i.e. cleaning the orifices, namely the genitals and anus, with water or stones. This is a mandatory practice and is one of the

---

[55] See: *'Rawa·i' at-Tibb al-Islaamiyy'* (1/72).

conditions of purification.[56] Allah praised the people of Quba village (in Madina) by saying:

$$\text{﴿ فِيهِ رِجَالٌ يُحِبُّونَ أَن يَتَطَهَّرُواْ وَٱللَّهُ يُحِبُّ ٱلْمُطَّهِّرِينَ ﴾}$$

Sura at-Tawbah; (9):108

[Meaning: In it are men who love to clean and to purify themselves.]

Ibn Al-Jawzi – may Allah have mercy upon him – said: "According to Ash-Sha'bi, the reason for the revelation of this verse was because some men from the village of Quba who used wash their private parts with water. Ibn 'Abbas said: When this verse was revealed, Allah's Messenger ﷺ went to them and asked: 'Why did Allah praise you?' They replied: 'We cleanse ourselves with water after answering the call of nature.'"[57]

Allah the Almighty created human beings in such a way that they naturally dispose of waste contained in their intestines and bladder through defecation and urination, respectively. This allows the human body to remain clean and healthy and facilitates the body's natural functions. Thus, after answering the call of nature, a Muslim must wash affected areas with water. In this regard, Prophet Muhammad ﷺ says: "Keep yourselves clean from urine, as majority of the

---

[56] See: *'Bahjat al-Abrar'* (p. 82).
[57] See: *'Zad al-Masir'* of Ibn al-Jawzi (3/501).

punishment in the grave is due to it."[58] i.e. purify and cleanse yourselves from it. This practice has great health benefits and modern medicine has proved that good genital hygiene protects the urinary tract from inflammations caused by the accumulation of germs and microbes. Likewise, it protects the anus from prostatitis, inflammations and abscesses. Those with chronic illnesses, especially diabetes, should ensure they clean themselves thoroughly due to high sugar levels in their urine which can increase risk of inflammation and purulence. These infections can be contracted by one's spouse during intercourse and may lead to permanent infertility.[59]

Furthermore, Islam recommends use of the left hand when cleaning impurities, so that the right hand, which is reserved for eating, remains clean and pure. Similarly, Islam enjoins that a person washes their hands after they finish using the toilet.

The concern Islam has for matters as small as this may be surprising to some people, however those who are aware of its magnitude and believe that it is the religion which Allah perfected and completed for mankind to follow until the Day of Resurrection are rather unsurprised. They know it is a way of life

---

[58] Reported by ad-Daruqutni (no. 7) and graded as authentic by al-Albani in 'Irwa· al-Ghalil' (no. 280).
[59] See: 'Asbab ash-Shifa· minal-Asqam wal-Ahwa·' (p. 35)

which contains nothing but good for Muslims who choose to follow it. Allah the Almighty says:

$$\left\{ \text{ٱلْيَوْمَ يَئِسَ ٱلَّذِينَ كَفَرُواْ مِن دِينِكُمْ فَلَا تَخْشَوْهُمْ وَٱخْشَوْنِ ٱلْيَوْمَ أَكْمَلْتُ لَكُمْ دِينَكُمْ وَأَتْمَمْتُ عَلَيْكُمْ نِعْمَتِى وَرَضِيتُ لَكُمُ ٱلْإِسْلَٰمَ دِينًا} \right\}$$

Sura al-Ma·idah; (5):3

[Meaning: This day those who disbelieve have despaired of defeating your religion; so, fear them not, but fear Me. This day I have perfected for you your religion and completed My favour upon you and have approved for you Islam as religion.]

The cleaning and removal of impurities prevents many illnesses and prevents the transmission of many contagious diseases by the permission of Allah.[60]

Abu Ishaq Al-'Iraqi writes in his book '*Asbab Ash-Shifa· Min Al-Asqam Wal-Ahwa·* (The Means to Cure Illness and Desires)': "A devastating typhoid outbreak occurred in the city of Aberdeen in Great Britain during 1964, causing terror in residents who frantically searched for a way to stop the epidemic from spreading. In the end, experts came to the solution of deciding to broadcast health instructions which ordered people to stop using paper towels and advised them to use water for cleaning instead.

---

[60] See: '*Asbab ash-Shifa· minal-Asqam wal-Ahwa·*' (p. 36).

Residents followed the advice, and amazingly, the infection stopped spreading and was contained. After witnessing the benefit of using water, the people adopted this practice as a habit instead of using toilet paper.

It is unknown how those residents would have reacted to the fact that this has been the practice of Muslims for over one-thousand four-hundred years, not because of a typhoid epidemic, but because the Creator of typhoid and other diseases commanded with all practices which promote health and wellbeing, and thus they continue to obey and comply. Allah the Almighty says:

Sura al-Mulk; (67):14 ﴿أَلَا يَعْلَمُ مَنْ خَلَقَ وَهُوَ ٱللَّطِيفُ ٱلْخَبِيرُ﴾

[Meaning: How could He who created not know His own creation, when He is the Most Subtle, the All Aware?][61]

10. Rinsing the mouth, i.e. swirling water around inside the mouth during ablution, in order to cleanse and purify it. Modern science has proven that rinsing the mouth protects it and the pharynx from inflammation, just as it protects the gums from purulence. This practice also cleans and protects the

---

[61] See: '*Asbab ash-Shifa· minal-Asqam wal-Ahwa*' (p. 36).

teeth as it removes food particles that gets stuck in the molars after eating.

Another benefit of rinsing the mouth is that it strengthens facial muscles and preserves facial shape and freshness. Sports professionals know the significance of this exercise which can bring about psychological calming in a person if they perfect the movement of their facial muscles when rinsing their mouths.[62]

Secondly: Regarding the prescription of ablution:

Ablution is a type of ritual washing involving the face, arms and legs. Washing these limbs is considered essential for the validity of this form of purification.

The ablution also has various recommended acts which are considered to enhance it. These include: Brushing the teeth prior to the performance of ablution; mentioning Allah's name at the time of performing ablution; washing the hands thrice at the beginning of ablution; rinsing the mouth thrice and expelling water from the nostrils thrice after snuffing it. It is also recommended at each stage of the ablution to start by washing with the right limb; running the fingers of one hand through the fingers of the other to

---

[62] See: 'Asbab ash-Shifa· minal-Asqam wal-Ahwa·' (p. 40).

ensure water reaches; wiping the ears and using a moderate amount of water.⁶³

Allah the Almighty says:

﴿ يَـٰٓأَيُّهَا ٱلَّذِينَ ءَامَنُوٓاْ إِذَا قُمۡتُمۡ إِلَى ٱلصَّلَوٰةِ فَٱغۡسِلُواْ وُجُوهَكُمۡ وَأَيۡدِيَكُمۡ إِلَى ٱلۡمَرَافِقِ وَٱمۡسَحُواْ بِرُءُوسِكُمۡ وَأَرۡجُلَكُمۡ إِلَى ٱلۡكَعۡبَيۡنِۚ ﴾

Sura Ma·idah; (5):6

[Meaning: O you who believe! When you intend to perform prayer, wash your faces and your forearms to the elbows and wipe over your heads and wash your feet to the ankles.]

Prophet Muhammad ﷺ said: "Allah does not accept the prayer of any of you who are in a state of impurity until you perform ablution."⁶⁴

Details regarding the performance of ablution occur in many Prophetic traditions and the scholars and jurists have discussed them at length. The intent here is not to describe the ablution, but to explain the link ablution has to hygiene and health. Some aspects concerning this relationship were covered in the previous subsection, however it is possible to add the following points:

1. Ablution is not merely washing the limbs and cleaning the body several times daily, rather the

---

⁶³ See: '*Fiqh as-Sunnah*' of Sayyid Sabiq (1/38).
⁶⁴ Reported by al-Bukhari (no. 6554) and Muslim (no. 225).

psychological effects and spiritual elevation felt by Muslims after performing ablution cannot be expressed in words, especially if a person fulfils it properly while being mindful of its merit. Thus, ablution has a profound impact on the life of Muslims and causes them to be refreshed, lively and radiant.[65]

2. Washing the limbs of ablution is considered to be an act of utmost importance for the promotion of hygiene and public health. Doctors say that these limbs are exposed to a huge number of microbes which are estimated to be in the region of several million per cubic centimetre of air. These microbes constantly attack the human body via exposed areas of skin, however during ablution they are totally swept from the surface of the skin and even more so when it is performed thoroughly as Allah's Messenger ﷺ instructed. In this way, no dirt or germs remain on the body after ablution apart from those which Allah decrees.[66]

3. Washing the face and the arms inclusive of the elbows during ablution has a greatly helps to rid the skin of dust, microbes and sweat, as well as cleansing it of sebum secreted by sebaceous glands. These

---

[65] See: '*Asbab ash-Shifa*·' (p. 39).
[66] See: '*Asbab ash-Shifa*·' (p. 41).

Health and Hygiene in Islam

elements form an optimal environment for germs to live and grow.[67]

4. Washing the feet thoroughly during ablution contributes to hygiene and causes a person to feel tranquillity, due to the influence of the feet on all body systems. This partly explains the tranquillity felt by a Muslim after performing ablution.[68]

5. It has been scientifically established that blood circulation is weaker in the upper limbs of the body, namely the hands and forearms, and the lower limbs of the body, namely the feet and legs, than in other parts of the body because they are the furthest from the heart which is the centre of the circulatory system. Therefore, washing these distal parts of the body during ablution improves blood circulation and hygiene in addition to invigorating and enlivening a person.

Additionally, it has been proven that the sun's rays and in particular, ultraviolet light, can cause cancer. However, this risk is greatly reduced by the performance of ablution as it ensures the surface of the skin is constantly moistened with water, especially areas of skin which are exposed to sunlight. Ablution

---

[67] See: *'Sahih Muslim'* with the explanation of an-Nawawi (1/105).
[68] See: *'Asbab ash-Shifa'* (p. 41).

thus protects the superficial and inner layers of skin from the harmful effects of solar radiation.[69]

Thirdly: Regarding the prescription of bathing

Bathing is the ritual washing of the whole body with water. Allah refers to it in the Quran in the following two verses:

﴿ وَإِن كُنتُمْ جُنُبًا فَٱطَّهَّرُوا۟ ﴾ Sura Ma·idah; (5):6

[Meaning: And if you are in a state of sexual impurity, then purify yourselves.]

﴿ وَيَسْـَٔلُونَكَ عَنِ ٱلْمَحِيضِ ۖ قُلْ هُوَ أَذًى فَٱعْتَزِلُوا۟ ٱلنِّسَآءَ فِى ٱلْمَحِيضِ ۖ وَلَا تَقْرَبُوهُنَّ حَتَّىٰ يَطْهُرْنَ ۖ فَإِذَا تَطَهَّرْنَ فَأْتُوهُنَّ مِنْ حَيْثُ أَمَرَكُمُ ٱللَّهُ ۚ إِنَّ ٱللَّهَ يُحِبُّ ٱلتَّوَّٰبِينَ وَيُحِبُّ ٱلْمُتَطَهِّرِينَ ﴾ Sura al-Baqarah; (2):222

[Meaning: And they ask you about menstruation. Say: "It is harm, so keep away from wives during menstruation. And do not approach them until they are pure. And when they have purified themselves, then come to them from where Allah has ordained for you. Indeed, Allah loves those who are constantly repentant, and He loves those who purify and cleanse themselves.]

---

[69] See: 'Asbab ash-Shifa·' (p. 41).

Bathing is well-known amongst all people. Humans throughout history have known the importance of bathing as a method of cleansing the body and curing many diseases. However, bathing has not been prescribed or systematised for any nation in history in the same way Allah has done for His final religion of Islam.

A researcher would have a very difficult job trying to compile the Islamic evidences mentioning bathing along with their scholarly explanations and would discover the greatness of Islam and the precision of its legislation.

In Islam, there are two broad types of bathing: obligatory and recommended. Bathing is obligatory upon conversion to Islam; after ejaculation or coitus, and at the end of menstruation and lochia. It is recommended, in the sense that its performance it meritorious but not essential, in the following cases: on Friday before Friday prayers; on the two days of Eid before the Eid prayers; before entering into the state of consecration for pilgrimage; upon entering Makkah, and for pilgrims on the day of 'Arafah.[70]

The benefits of bathing are the same as those of ablution, however bathing is more effective in cleaning and better in terms of hygiene.

---

[70] See: *'Sahih Muslim'* with the explanation of an-Nawawi (1/219-36) & *'Fiqh as-Sunnah'* of Sayyid Sabiq (1/59-66).

Fourthly: Islamic texts promoting public health

There are numerous references to public health in Islamic religious texts concerning cleanliness of homes, public places, clothing, etc. The following is a non-exhaustive list of the narrations in this regard:

1. Removing harmful objects from roads is one of the branches of faith. On the authority of Abu Hurairah – may Allah be pleased with him – that Prophet Muhammad ﷺ said: "Faith has seventy-odd branches or sixty-odd branches, the uppermost of which is the declaration: 'None has the right to be worshipped except Allah'; and the least of which is the removal of harmful objects from the road.. And modesty is a branch of faith."[71]

2. Urinating in standing water is prohibited. On the authority of Jabir – may Allah be pleased with him – that Prophet Muhammad ﷺ forbade urinating in stagnant water.[72] In a similar narration, Abu Hurairah – may Allah be pleased with him – relates the saying of the Prophet ﷺ: "You should not urinate in still water that does not flow and then use it to wash."[73]

These two narrations prohibit urination in standing water in order to prevent it from becoming contaminated and impure for people to use. The

---

[71] Reported by al-Bukhari (no. 9) and Muslim (no. 35).
[72] Reported by Muslim (no. 281).
[73] Reported by al-Bukhari (no. 239) & Muslim (no. 282).

prohibition of defecation in standing water and of cleaning oneself after answering the call of nature using standing water is also inferred from these narrations.[74]

3. Bathing in standing water is prohibited according to the narration on the authority of Abu Hurairah – may Allah be pleased with him – who said: 'Allah's Messenger ﷺ said: "None of you should bathe in standing water when you are in a state of sexual impurity." One of the narrators asked Abu Hurairah: 'Then what should such a person do, O Abu Hurairah?' He replied: 'They should take some out and then use it.'[75]

The foregoing has been a brief overview of the importance of hygiene in Islam.

---

[74] See: '*Tawdih al-Ahkam*' (1/129).
[75] Reported by Musim (no. 283).

www.ingramcontent.com/pod-product-compliance
Lightning Source LLC
LaVergne TN
LVHW021049100526
838202LV00079B/5409